Koans for the Inner Dog
A Guide to Canine Enlightenment

Cosmo
muse and teacher
Circa 2000

Koans for the Inner Dog
A Guide to Canine Enlightenment

LLyn De Danaan

Hypatia-in-the-Woods Press
Printed by Gorham Printing 2003

Hypatia-in-the-Woods Press
160 Southeast Lagoon Lane
Shelton, Washington 98584

Book and Cover Design
Llyn De Danaan

First Edition: October 2003
Printed in the United States of America

Library of Congress Catalogue Number
2003096500
ISBN 0-9705961-3-8

"Listen my friend. There is one thing in the world that satisfies, and that is meeting with the Dog."
Nate, fifteenth century Rottweiler poet and Sufi

Dedicated to all my dog teachers:
Mac, Frances, Kinky Reeker,
Fred, and Russell.

Special dedication to Belle,
Cosmo's friend
and walking companion.

Contents

"Experience teaches us that many things gain by not being completely seen, but veiled and concealed."
Jacob Cats,
Mirror of the Old and New Time,
1627

"But then, what does a cat know?"
Cosmo, Spaniel skeptic, 2003

"You can preach a better sermon with your bark than with your bite."

Shad Mimms, Cocker Spaniel theologian
and associate member,
Risen Faith Fellowship, 2003

Preface

What is a Koan?

A koan represents a principle that has a spiritual foundation. These principles are illustrated by way of short stories or vignettes that must be studied for their truths to be revealed. A koan depicts a situation or a moment of learning. A koan is a tool for teaching insight. The insight cannot be achieved by logic but by a kind of AHA! or conversion experience. The study of koans encourages the mind to see every situation, every moment, as a koan. The study of koans encourages the mind to reflect upon all of life's experience before acting. This collection of koans is one that will be of value to the dog who seeks to resolve the dilemmas of his or her own existence.

Organization of the Book

Part I of the book provides a general discussion on the spiritual development of the dog. I recommend that the dog and his or her human companion read this section aloud together, perhaps one chapter a week, before beginning the study of the koans in Part II.

Preparation

It may be useful to have an exercise mat for both human and dog as well as a couple of very fluffy zazen cushions. Try these out before purchasing. Be sure that the dog's cushion has a removable, washable cover.

How can a Dog Benefit from Studying Koans?

Any dog can benefit from the study of koans. A dog will become keener, more alive to each moment, and more joyful. A dog who studies koans will learn to seek peace within him or herself, to understand his or her inner nature, and to be in charge of his or her anger. A dog who studies koans will lead his human companion to a place of compassion and love.

One/Introduction

"No leash will ever restrain
my imagination"
Nineteenth Century,
Anonymous

"Mick was on his game: graceful, powerful, self-possessed to the point of cockiness. Only after the best- in- show judge, Irene Biven, named him victor did he rear up and begin to shadowbox with his handler, revealing his inner brat."
Sean Kelly, on Westminster Champion Kerry Blue,
New York Times, February 16, 2003

"It is never true that the bark is worse than the bite. A bite is always worse and is spiritually dangerous for the biter"

Foxy, Akita poet and painter, 2003

The Foundation of Dog Soul:
The Hundred Year Old Dog Within

Does a dog have a soul? We know what a dog is. What is a soul? Let us decide that it is the spiritual aspect of a living creature. Let us imagine that it is the part of a creature that is capable of happiness or sorrow; that it is the part of a creature that can suffer or experience delight. Let us imagine that this part of a creature can exist beyond the end of the physical manifestation of the creature, that is, after breath has left the body, after the heart has ceased to beat, and after the point at which cells begin to deteriorate. Clearly a dog is capable of happiness, of sorrow, of suffering and delight. A dog's happiness is palpable. A dog responds eagerly to a long walk, a new squeaky toy, a hoof to chew upon, a scruff behind the ears, a warm lap, or a bed by the hearth. These all bring joy. But does a dog's spiritual being live on beyond its death? It is just as likely that a dog's being continues as a human's. In fact, given the inherent goodness of almost every dog, it seems more likely that a dog's soul be granted eternal life if such is granted to anything. Whether it is called soul or spirit or anything else, what is clear is that dogs have access to *The Hundred Year Old Dog Within* (hereafter referred to as *THYODW*). This dog energy, spirit, or archetype is available to all dogs if they know how to find and talk with it. *THYODW* is the bearer of the accumulated experience of dogs in the world. This hundred year old dog is a wisdom figure. It is the dog within who knows how to raise a pup, how to please a human, how to hunt and fetch, and how to beg from under the table.

It is the dog within who has the capacity for endless love and incredible sacrifice. It is the dog within who is the dreamer and the dreamed, who informs the waking dog of his or her responsibility, and guides his or her choices.

It is this dog within who can be awakened with the study of the koans. She/he is always there, always ready, but not always accessible. The prepared pup, the vigilant pup, the seeking pup, will find *THYODW* with patience and the assistance of his or her human companion.

Exercise for Dogs

Roll over. Get into a comfortable position, preferably away from distractions such as cats, cat food, or tennis balls. Lie down. If there is anything still in your way, leave it.

Close your eyes. Let your breath come slowly in and out. If anything comes to mind, notice it and let it go. Drop it. Leave it.

Now picture the most perfect dog you can. Breed does not matter. Just see this dog as clearly as possible.. See its fur, the color of its fur, the shape and size of the tail, the shape of the head, the way the ears are attached to the head. Notice its eyes. See the muzzle. Do not growl. Just notice.

Now imagine you are approaching this dog. You sniff each other in all the prescribed places. There is nothing threatening here. Breathe easily and imagine yourself sitting in front of this dog, neither submissive nor aggressive. Just be there.

Sit.. Lie Down.

Now ask this dog to guide you in your quest to be an enlightened, good dog. This is your inner dog. Once you have discovered it, you will be able to talk with him or her anytime you choose.

A note to human companions: You may need to talk your dog through this exercise several times before he or she is able to have access to the inner dog. Make an audio tape of the instructions so that the dog may play it while you are away from the house or otherwise occupied. This is, of course, not the ideal. We would hope you could give your time to this valuable enterprise and "companion" your dog along the journey.

Neither of you should be discouraged by initial failures. The inner dog exercise will eventually prepare your dog to hear the koans more clearly and to have spiritual guidance in applying them to his or her life.

Multiple Intelligences and the Dog[1]

"Oh, to have multiple intelligences." This is the lament of the dog who doesn't realize that she or he already has them. In fact, most dogs have more intelligences than most humans. Multiple intelligences was a term coined by Howard Gardner, a professor of cognition and education at Harvard Graduate School of Education.. Of course, a Harvard professor would be surrounded, or think he was, by lots of intelligence. Gardner began to see that not all of this intelligence was of the same ilk. Plus he noticed that most of the schools in the United States emphasized language or linguistic intelligence and logical-mathematical intelligence. Indeed, we know that many young children are drilled in numbers and letters. Few contemporary youngsters are taught to appreciate visual arts or to learn the color and shape of leaves. So those who are gifted in these ways are neglected, he said. In fact, he believed, it is those with such gifts who are sometimes called "learning disabled."

Gardner didn't really know much about dogs. Gardner's theories, however, are useful in understanding the full potential of the dog's mind and body. First, we must clearly distinguish intelligence from instinct. Many who do not understand dogs believe that dogs operate primarily from instinct. They train and teach according to this misapprehension.

Granted, instinct informs the repetitive, basic task of survival in an unchanging world. Instinct serves the dog well.

The problem with instinct is that the world is always changing. Intelligences allow for adaptation to changing circumstances. All dogs are endowed with intelligences. Some may be latent. Others are simply underdeveloped. A dog, left alone, may be able to recognize certain abilities on his or her own and find ways to enhance these. A dog, with a good human companion and the aid of koans and other exercises suggested in this book, will, without question, have access to more intelligences and be able to apply them to daily life.

If a human companion understands the theory and language of multiple intelligences, he or she will notice that dogs who are "trained" with mere words are deprived of the opportunity to develop spatial intelligence, bodily-kinesthetic intelligence, musical intelligence, interpersonal intelligence, and naturalist intelligence. They are unfairly limited and often judged stupid. And yet dogs are born with all of these intelligences! Give your dog full rein to select his or her own direction and unique way of moving and sensing. Do not fear the mess that may be made. Do not fear the loss of control. That's part of the deal. Humans, do not fear that your neighbors and friends will think you mad. They will. Dogs need opportunities to judge how far away a ball will land and how high a frisbee will fly, for example. Dogs need opportunities to listen to music and respond to pitch and tone of musically offered commands. Humans must try singing little ditties to their dogs. An invitation to a meal can be enhanced when set to a melody your dog friend enjoys. Dogs need time to relate to other dogs and other humans. Dogs need to have the opportunity to smell and urinate on all kinds of foliage. They will appreciate being given the time to notice the difference between and among grasses and sedges, ornamentals and native specimens as they take their evening stroll.

Whatever you are teaching, whichever koan you are reading together, think of these multiple intelligences and how they can be used in an approach to learning. Allow deep play. Embrace it.

The Senses of the Dog

The senses of the dog, as you are aware, come fully excited. There is nothing banal about the world in which a dog lives. Every moment brings a feeling, a touch, a scent, a new experience of the world. A bit of cracker hidden in the leaf litter at the base of an alder tree is just as liable to create interest as the ruffle of one's fur in a sudden breeze, or the sight of a bufflehead duck rising from the water on a fall day. A dog knows about the senses.

However, a dog must learn to discern between and among stimuli that awaken senses. The act of discernment requires judgment and keen insight. What is the difference between the duck and the cracker? Which is good? Which is evil? How is a dog to know?

Rules for the Development of Dog Discernment[2]

1. Enjoy the world of senses. Take joy in smell, touch, and taste. Recognize that however sad you may be about something in your life, your lively senses will relieve the suffering.

2. There is no rhyme or reason to it. Don't try to figure out why your senses bring such joy. Just be there with them.

3. But, and here's the pinch, sometimes the things that seem to bring you joy can be really bad for you. Your senses can fool you into doing something you may live to regret.

4. You can really get into trouble if the smell of the neighbor's garbage overwhelms your intention to be a good dog.

5. You must notice your joy, but also follow the thoughts and intentions that accompany this joy. You have got to learn to notice when you are distracted, or when you are about to do something that is less good than what your dog soul has intended for you to do. Believe me, your peace and tranquility will suffer if you knock over that garbage can and eat the stuff that scatters about on the ground. It will seem really yummy at first. But the consequences, my friend, are not worth it.

6. Okay, imagine that you have knocked over the can. All is not lost. Try to notice and recall the steps that led up to this act. Remember, step by step, the feelings of excitement and joy, the temptation presented, the moment of stepping over the line. By this means, you will begin to help yourself to guard against future transgressions.

7. The disposition of the dog is positive. The tendency always is to be good. Notice your senses, notice your inclinations toward the bad. You will become sweeter and sweeter.

8. Console yourself. Do not judge yourself harshly. The dog soul will develop with love and attention through a consortium with good spirited dogs who are also on the path, and through the practice of healthy habits and joyful resolutions to be awake!

Breath as a Sixth Sense or Why Dogs Pant

Panting is a way of extending all of the senses. Any human who is a connoisseur knows that to truly appreciate a fine wine, all senses must be awakened. One looks at color including the "rim" color of the wine. One swirls the wine in order to observe the body of the wine. One smells the wine, placing one's nose deep within the glass. Usually one is guided to take a quick whiff for first impression, followed by a deep full- lunged inward snort. One notices impressions. Then comes taste.

The tongue is a very delicate and highly specialized instrument. Human taste buds can detect the differences among sweet, salty, sour, and bitter tastes. Some buds are in the front, some in the back of the human tongue. Wine tasters take a first sip, then slosh wine around on to a rolled tongue and draw air over it. The air drawn across the tongue gives the fullest, richest experience of the wine.

A dog's tongue is even more specialized than that of a human. However, dog takes in initial impressions from the eyes, then swirls his own body around the environment, sometimes running a mad pace in great circles in order to stir up all that is to be experienced. He cannot, you see, swirl the yard or the park, so he must swirl himself. He whiffs here and there, at first tentatively and then in great gulps. At last, he begins to pant. The pant is done, correctly, with the tongue hanging out. Great drafts of air are pulled in and out of the mouth and lungs and across the sensitive tongue. In this way dog fully experiences the overall flavor of a place, a day, and a moment in time. Dog fully tastes his day in this way. Without the pant, dog is experiencing only partially what there is around him. Dog tongue is not merely attuned to tastes such as sweet and sour, but to duck and goose, deer and squirrel, positive human energy, and primordial fear. The dog tongue has zones of acceptance and zones of resistance as well as zones of pleasure/ approach and danger/avoidance.

Awakening Dog Chi

A fully aroused and properly attuned dog tongue is able to awaken dog chi. That's because a fully aroused dog tongue allows the dog to become a fully functioning being. Lao Tzu said that the way to appreciate life is to apprehend everything through being, rather than acting. Dogs are able to do this because they are not compelled to act except under very special circumstances. They do not think about the need to serve on committees or to improve their bodies by going to gyms. They don't think they must go to church to be better dogs. They usually don't hold down jobs or make payments on houses. They don't have credit cards or other debts. They don't get in cars and drive around mindlessly seeking new places or new thrills. So a dog has a better crack at being, just being. But a dog can benefit by increasing the flow of energy _in_ its being. The concept of chi energy is a very complex and old one and this is not the proper venue for an exhaustive discussion of it. Suffice it to say that chi energy flows through the body and its quality is determined by the kind of life a dog leads. A dog who eats well, drinks plenty of water, breathes deeply, and pants regularly will keep the chi circulating. Circulating chi will help the dog stay in balance both physically and emotionally.

Kundalini and the Dog

The dog does, however, have access to even more energy. Of course, human beings who know dogs have noticed that many dogs wag their tails under certain circumstances. Experts have written that the purpose of this wag is to stimulate a gland located in the anal region. This gland will then emit an odor that marks the dog's territory. This is all very well and good and indeed is the manifest function of wagging and a function that those who do not understand the complex spiritual nature of the dog are happy to accept without further examination.

The latent function of wagging is far more significant. The root of the tail is the location of primal energy in dogs as well as humans. Ancient philosophies call this the kundalini center. The tail root at the base of the spine gives energy and vitality to the entire being. A dog who has not studied kundalini, but comes to wagging naturally, may be shocked to learn that there is, in fact, a snake coiled tightly around this tail root. This is not a very big snake. It is not a dangerous snake unless awakened in the context of the baser energies. It is a snake that can be awakened by wagging. Without wagging, the snake lies dormant and sleeping. Without wagging fiercely and at correct times, the dog may remain fearful and lethargic. Basset Hounds, as a breed, could use with more wagging, for example. Jack Russells could do with a little less.

How to Awaken Tail Energy

Lie Down

Now assume the doggy pose, rear end elevated above your mat and front paws stretched out as far as you can manage. This will put your head close to the ground. Some humans call this a "play bow" and have seen it as an invitation that dogs extend to humans, dogs, and even inanimate objects, to engage in games. Of course, this interpretation of the doggy pose is incorrect. So many things said about dogs are incorrect. The pose is meant to initiate a *tail energy* session. Dogs enjoy practice with others and are often testing the spiritual development of friends and companions. To my human readers: the best way to respond to a dog who takes the doggy pose in your presence is to fall to your own mat and assume the pose yourself. Let the dog lead you through the exercises.

Now then, in the doggy pose, with the upper half of the body fully stretched out in front, buttocks in the air, and the tail held high off the buttocks, begin a slow wag. Move the tail slowly so as not to strain or harm the tail. Begin the wag at the tip of the tail and move it downward toward your rump until the root is engaged. Keep the spine aligned to the tail. The path from your neck and chest up to your tail root should be straight. Hold the pose as you wag more rapidly. Wag vigorously now from this position for five minutes.

For the older dog: if necessary, you may use squeaky balls, pillows, stuffed animals, or furniture to help to achieve and hold the pose.

Practice taking the pose and wagging several times a day, whenever you think about it. Try it in new places so that you don't get bored with it.

Once you have mastered the doggy pose and are able to wag for five minutes, try combining it with a good pant.

For the advanced student: Place a neon tennis ball directly in front of your nose while assuming the pose and panting. Stare at it.

Running or Walking: Which is Spiritually Correct For You?

Unless disabled or injured through accident, a dog is a four-legged creature. This four-leggedness differentiates the dog from the two-legged, the finned, and the winged creatures of earth. There are many ways to develop and celebrate four-leggedness. It is useful for dog to assess his or her own approach to four-leggedness and reflect upon the meaning of that approach. Each dog has a leggedness that both mirrors and informs his or her personality, food preference, and approach to spiritual development.

Basic Leg Nature Types[3]

The walker. This type is characterized by slow, deliberate movement. This type is usually more at home with the older human and in an urban or suburban setting. The walker is never airborne. The impact of movement on the skeletal structure is minimal. There is time for contemplation and enjoyment of surroundings. The walker often stops abruptly to sniff around bushes and lampposts. Is just as happy to stay home and read the paper. Sometimes employed in airport baggage areas.

The trotter. Two or more feet may be occasionally airborne. The head is often moving to and fro as the trotter takes in his or her environment. The trotter is a proud, almost cocky dog. If on leash, he or she must often be reminded not to pull. Easily distracted. Often has a short, wide head. Fully domesticated. A short neck and shrill bark sometimes present. Cannot keep quiet when left in a parked car. Impulse to be a "ham." Often cast in television sit-coms.

The runner. This dog is at home in the country

or open meadows. Often airborne. Very good at taking hurdles in agility meets. Difficulty in describing, at the end of the day, what he or she has actually seen . Big teeth, long neck, and thick bones often present. This dog is highly competitive and sometimes neglects the big picture in favor of the race well run. This type is featured in lots of dog food commercials.

The lunger. This type can be very happy to walk until a squirrel or another dog is seen. At this point, the dog makes a sudden forward move. The impulse begins in the hindquarters and most of the stress is on the back legs and feet. The dog's body is propelled forward and is often airborne for a moment before actually making contact with the victim. The intended victim, if it escapes up a tree, is tracked and glared at from below, sometimes for hours. This dog leads an active fantasy life. This is often the dog that twitches while sleeping.

The springer. This type is confined to one breed of dog and the antelope. The dog rarely makes contact with the ground, instead "springing" off all four feet and propelling him or herself forward five to eight feet at a bound. This type is associated with manic circle dances and suprisingly long, breathtaking "hang times." Sometimes a springer seems to walk on air. Exhibits a high degree of clownish behavior with toys. This type is forever young, a Peter Pan of dogs. Is fascinated with human beings and situates him or herself in a location to observe them when not springing.

Eight Tests for Determining your Leg Nature Type

It is essential that you understand your *leg nature type* in order to exercise properly. Answer the simple questions below and rate yourself accordingly. Please just answer with the first thing that comes to mind. Do not deliberate or discuss the questions. It is preferable to take the test without the help of a human companion.

It is likely that some dogs will lie on tests such as these in order to please a human. This will decidedly skew the results.

Read each question carefully and check boxes

true or false. It may be useful for you to write a few comments after answering each question. You may find that the questions stimulate particular memories for you. Or you may be aware of ways in which you have modified your natural behavior in order to please a particularly insistent or controlling human. Just make note of these thoughts and move to the next question.

The questions:
1. When given the option of staying home or riding along in the backseat of a car on a trip of unknown destination, I opt for the ride. True ☐ False ☐ Comments:

2. After a walk or run, followed by a bowl of water and a snack, I am ready for more. True ☐ False ☐
Comments:

3. I use my bark rarely and only when something really bizarre happens in the neighborhood.
True ☐ False ☐
Comments:

4. I often fantasize chasing rabbits. In my

dreams, nothing can stop me. True ☐ False ☐
Comments:

5. When I see a squirrel hopping about the yard, I stake it out and plan a strategy for overcoming it. True ☐ False ☐ Comments:

6. I am not fooled by duck decoys. True ☐ False ☐
Comments:

7. I pretend to be extremely obedient but when no one is watching, I jump up on counter tops and lick all the plates that haven't been washed yet.
True ☐ False ☐ Comments:

8. No matter how often I am corrected, I continue to jump on people who come to visit. True ☐ False ☐
Comments:

Scoring:
If you answered two or fewer questions true, you are a walker.

If you answered three questions true, you are a trotter.

If you answered four questions true, you are a runner.

If you answered five questions true you are a lunger.

If you answered six to eight true, you are, without doubt, a springer.

Once you have determined your *leg nature type* you can develop an appropriate exercise routine.

Walkers Lie down. Stay. Start with the pads of your feet. Feel each pad individually. Now tense the pads then relax them. Alternate which foot you begin with. Practice tensing and relaxing until you can feel the difference. Work your way up the muscles surrounding the metacarpals, the ulna, the elbow and the humerus on the front legs. Then move to the back legs and tense the muscles surrounding the tarsus, the fibula, the tibia, and the femur. Tense your shoulders then move to the pelvic area. Repeat this exercise of tensing and relaxing muscle groups each day as you lie about the house dreaming.

Trotters Find a quiet place away from all distractions. Lie down. Visualize yourself decorated with flowers and beautifully combed, like a Chinese lion dog. Visualize yourself moving deliberately and carefully along the polished marble floors of a grand palace. See yourself avoiding an embarrassing slip. See your legs carrying you proudly and upright toward a bowl of chopped livers. See your legs as strong, powerful, and absolutely trustworthy.

Runners. If your human companion has a treadmill, borrow it or arrange a time that you may use it each day. Put on a compact disc with music. Jazz is good. Jessica Williams' *All Alone* album is terrific. Clip the safety switch of the treadmill to your collar. Start at a reasonable pace and then increase the pace and the elevation each day. You should be able to sustain a pant producing, energy awakening run while listening to Jessica at the piano. Do not wag during this exercise. It is not the goal of the run to awaken the kundilini energy. The run should, however, increase dog chi and appreciation of jazz piano.

Lungers. Find or buy a miniature trampoline. Place it in your yard. Place three foot high hurdles approximately four feet away from it on two opposite sides. Practice running hard at a hurdle, clearing it, hitting the trampoline, and then springing over the second hurdle. Do this five times a day until you are exhausted. Eat moderately in order to maintain a lean profile. Listen to John Phillip Sousa when possible.

Springers. You don't need any exercises.

The Limitations of your Human Companion and Leg Nature

If you are reading this book, you are already aware of your particular human companion's limitations. Obviously, we hope that you have chosen a human that is correct for your *leg nature type*. A walker can make do with a lethargic, contemplative type. A runner needs to choose a human with lots of endurance and stamina. Many the dog has found him or herself stuck with a human that simply doesn't match his or her *leg nature type*. It is possible, sometimes, to work with a human. One must address him or her head on and not allow bad habits to persist.

However, let there be no doubt. Humans are very hard to change especially after they are about two months old.

A walker and a springer enjoying a winter stroll. It is possible for dogs with different leg natures to accommodate one another and often find it advantageous to do so. Here they both pace themselves for the convenience of a two year old human companion.

Developing a Signature Bark:
An Exercise In Channeling Anger
and Creating Beauty

There was a dog who pulled on his leash and barked and barked and barked to be let free. He wanted badly to go forth on his own and race about with other dogs. Every day when he and his human companion went out for a walk, he pulled. Every evening during the otherwise pleasant twilight strolls, he pulled. Finally, in exasperation, he asked the master: "When will you let me be free to romp and play with all the other dogs in the parks and meadows?" The master answered, "You will be free when you have overcome your eagerness to be free."

All the tugging and pulling and incessant barking were getting the dog nowhere. He had not conquered his aggressive will to explode into the world. He had not found peace within. He had not come to understand that his way of entering the world was mindless and could only lead to trouble for him and for everyone around him.

Barking itself can be aggressive and may be misunderstood if used as an opening ploy in a

A young dog becoming familiar with the bark apparatus. It is never too early to begin daily practice.

conversation. Barking is often seen by humans as a negative thing. Thousands of dollars are spent by humans on trying to stop dogs from barking. There are anti-barking collars, anti-barking sprays, and books about anti-barking. But barking is a perfectly natural component of a dog's communication tool kit. Birds sing, frogs croak, humans use words. The dog, like his cousin wolf, barks. The bark is useful. It is the fussy suburban or urbanites, who have no business having companion dogs, who try to suppress the bark. A bark warns, spreads news, announces, and conveys the deepest felt emotions. A dog without a bark is a sorry dog indeed.

Bark Theory

The bark may be thought of as an extremely flexible instrument of communication. Though the lips, teeth, and tongue are the parts of the body most obviously involved, in fact there is much more involved in producing a good bark. The lungs, of course, provide the air for the bark. The larynx, with the vocal folds, produces the bark itself. The folds vibrate as the air from the lungs pass over them. The space between the folds is called the glottis. Folds that move freely and are well tuned are not unlike the strings of a violin or cello. The pharynx and oral cavity act as resonators and amplify the bark. Bigger resonators produce bigger, deeper barks. The nose, even, is important. The moist nose warms the air taken into the lungs and the snout/nose combo amplify the bark.. A good long snout, a full moist nose, and a nice long, supple neck, unrestricted, we might well caution, by tight collars, assures a fine bark.

The diaphragm makes it possible to sustain a long howl or rapid series of breath free barks. A dog should work to control the diaphragm and thus control his or her breath more precisely.

Practice Makes Perfect

A dog, however, must learn to hone the bark for maximum effectiveness. A truly practiced and disciplined dog will develop a *signature bark* that is his or hers alone. How is this done?

First, a dog must practice vocalizations until he or she becomes familiar with his or her apparatus and comfortable with the sounds that can be made with it. The dog must take deep breaths, shoulders back, throat relaxed, and howl his or her way up and down the scales. This can be done anywhere, but if you have a fussy or timid human, you may want to go into a closed room and play loud music to mask your exercises. Remove or loosen any collars before beginning.

These exercises will help the dog to explore his or her full bark potential. Practice opening and closing the glottis with puffs of air and long streams of air. See if you can do this without exerting yourself too much. Try high pitch yelps then blood curdling shrieks. Try "bending" a howl up and then down until you are satisfied that you've got a good handle on what your bark can do. Humans may find all of this annoying.

After becoming familiar with your range, notice what tones feel best in your throat. Some dogs' vocal chords are clearly relaxed within certain ranges, while they are strained or stressed in others. Once you have found a range in which your chords feel relaxed, notice which tones simply sound right to you.

When you have selected three or four tones, try using them in a tattoo fashion, that is, snapping the tones out forcefully in a regular rhythmic beat. You may wish to tap one paw to keep the rhythm steady. Repeat this over and over every chance you get. Practice in locked cars when your human companion has left you parked while he or she is shopping. Practice when your human companion leaves you alone at home. Practice when someone new comes into the yard. This will give you a good chance to see if your particular bark is recognized and acknowledged.

For the Advanced Dog

After you've gotten really good at short, staccato barks, try some variations. Try barking without pausing for breath over a five to ten minute period. Join in barking marathons with other neighborhood dogs.

If you practice regularly, you will, indeed, develop your own unique and special *signature bark*. People all over your neighborhood will recognize it.

Barking vs. Snarling

Barking is to be differentiated from snarling. We will take up the growl later. But a word about snarling is appropriate in conjunction with this discussion on the bark. Some dogs have learned to snarl automatically when they see something or someone new, strange, unusual, or out of place. They believe that the snarl will head off any need for real confrontation and give them a head start in the event of an actual fight. Indeed, it is the fight for which they salivate. This belief has been capitalized upon and touted widely by its adherents. It has become popular among angry, unhealed dogs and has even entered the arena of human foreign policy decisions. Some humans, amazingly enough, are willing to take advice from quite odd quarters.

Preemptive snarling, is, however, and make no mistake about it, a spiritual trap. It comes from a deep need to hurt. Dogs who promote this practice have typically been taken away from their litter too early. Sometimes they come from very large litters and did not receive enough personal attention and nourishment as pups. Sometimes they have spent too much time in kennels or crates during the early months of their lives. They have not had the experience of empathetic, kind parenting, and have little trust for other dogs or humans. In short, these dogs have been morally, symbolically "bitten" and are out to "bite" someone else. Because they snarl and bite, they are snarled at. This return snarl or bite affirms their belief that the world is all bad. They are trapped spiritually and emotionally in the cycle that psychologists call "narcissistic injury." It is possible to escape the trap. It is best not to fall into it to begin with. Learn to bark without anger. Learn to watch and wait. Learn to notice the differences between a friendly, curious approach and a threatening one. Try everything else before going for the throat.

Growling for Spiritual Growth

Like anything else, growling can be used for good or bad. Even good growling can be over done. A dog must use judgment in deciding when to growl. It takes time to develop this judgment, but with time, all dogs of goodwill will apply the growl correctly. Be careful. An overused growl will affect the vocal chords negatively and the *signature bark* may suffer.

It is all right to growl at:

♦ Children who throw stones at you

♦ People who do not recycle

♦ People who take long showers

♦ People who make racist remarks
   or seek to exclude

- People who throw garbage out
  the windows of cars
- Things that scare you in the
  night
- Disrespectful cats

This is not to be an aggressive or threatening growl, but one that releases the anger within and acts as a gentle reproach. This is not a self-righteous growl. One must be careful not to fall into the trap of feeling "better than." Each growl has a lesson to teach. Listen to yourself and what the growl is telling you. The impulse to growl tells you something about what is not right in the world. Don't ignore it.

*Every dog takes the limits of his own field of vision for
the limits of the world. That's
why some dogs simply cannot find a tennis ball once it
goes into the bushes.*

Art Schnauzer, Westminster nay sayer and
philosopher, 2001

Two/The Koans

狗

I. Noticing Waves

A dog visiting the seashore for the first time ran gleefully toward the water. Yet when she arrived at where the water had been, there was only very wet sand. As she stood staring at her own footprints and a plenitude of sand dollars, a great wave washed over her. She ran as quickly as she could further up the beach, half drowned and soaked to the skin. She turned around and the water was gone again. This, she concluded, was not a lake.

狗

II. Things Could be Worse

A dog had a large bone. She kept it with her at all times. When another dog approached, she growled. When a human approached she growled. She carried the bone to her bed and only half slept so she would be aware if anyone came near to steal the bone. She carried the bone with her to her food dish and gulped her kibble because she feared letting the bone out of her mouth for more than a few moments. She desired the bone. She possessed the bone. But this bone brought her nothing but misery. One day, quite by accident, she dropped the bone. It fell into a very deep hole. She could not retrieve it. For a day or two, she was anxious and plotted ways to get the bone back. But then, one morning, she awoke and noticed the sun rising. She had let go of her burdensome possession. She finally learned to have more by coming to desire less.

狗

III. You are not your Growl[4]

A despairing dog had no friends to speak of. He thought that he must growl and lunge at everything and everyone if he were to be appreciated as a truly important dog in the world. The dog finally heard the message of nonviolence and became benign. He no longer growled or barked or lunged at trespassers in threatening ways. It did not take long for some nasty neighborhood children to realize that the dog was not a danger to them. They laughed at it and tossed rocks at it and teased it unmercifully. The dog did not understand that nonviolence does not require that one absorb the violence of others.

狗

IV. Shaking Paws

One day a woman came visiting. She was smitten by the dog who lived in the house of her friend. She tried very hard to teach the dog to shake hands. She held out a treat and implored, "Give me your paw." She poked the dog's thigh to encourage him. She lifted the paw with her own hand to show what she wanted. She tried over and over. But the dog would not lift his paw to her. He did, happily, eat the treats she held out for him. As soon as the woman went home, the dog approached his human companion and lifted one paw to her.

狗

V. Mud

A dog followed a raccoon. He chased it round and round in circles in the woods. The raccoon ran to the beach. It was a low tide. The raccoon easily balanced on the slippery mud. The dog followed but being considerably heavier than the raccoon , sank to his elbows. He could not get back to shore.

狗

VI. Bad Dogs[5]

Four dogs in training were left in a house for the evening. They were told to stay out of the kitchen as part of the test of their obedience. At first they were very good and did not even look at the kitchen. Then around midnight one could stand it no longer. She entered the kitchen, sniffed around for a minute, then snatched a piece of ham that had been left on the counter. A second dog, watching all this, ran into the kitchen and snapped the ham from the mouth of the first. He swallowed it without chewing. The third dog came into the kitchen and began licking crumbs from the linoleum as he scolded "You are bad dogs. Why did you enter the kitchen?" Upon hearing this the fourth dog opened the refrigerator saying smugly, "It looks as if I am the only dog who hasn't disobeyed. I am a very good dog."

狗

VII. Stay Focused[6]

A dog wondered about cats. She watched them and worried about them. One day she asked her human companion, "Master, can a cat become enlightened? It seems so impossible to me." The master replied, "Why do you want to discuss the enlightenment of cats? The question is how you can become enlightened. Think about that."

狗

VIII. Mindless Barking

A dog was so excited by everything that he spent each day barking and howling. He went about his yard barking. He visited neighbors barking. He barked at deer and cats and raccoons. He barked at the postal carrier. He barked at the meter reader. One day his human companion said, "I wish you would stop all this barking. There is no end to all this announcement of your presence, this calling attention to yourself." The dog was immediately enlightened.

IX. Bread Mantra

A dog had been stealing bread from the kitchen counter. When her human companions came home, they found whole loaves of bread devoured and ripped plastic bread wrappers strewn carelessly about the house.

The dog was punished every day. One day the people came home to find the dog, on a braided rug, staring at an unopened loaf lying just inches from her nose. She had been enlightened in the middle of her act of thievery.

X. Why?

A dog confined in a kennel or locked in a car is more dangerous to himself and others than a dog running loose.

狗

XI. The Essential Dog

A lively dog caught his tail in a swinging door. It was so mangled it had to be removed. Another spunky pup, after a serious bout of barking, could no longer bark. A friend of this dog was attacked by a rascally bobcat she had been tracking. She lost her right back leg. Yet another dog lost her tail, could not bark ever, and was missing a tooth. No one ever took these animals to be anything but dogs.

狗

XII. A Dog Heard but not Seen

A dog sat on her porch every morning. Each day as a walker passed by on the street she barked. She barked when she first saw a person. She barked when the person walked in front of her porch. She barked until the person was out of sight. One day a walker stopped and looked deeply into the dog's eyes. The barking stopped. The dog thought to herself, "At last someone has heard me."

狗

XIII. Let Sleeping Dogs Lie

A dog swore that she had not made off with her master's breakfast though there were traces of granola and yogurt all around her muzzle and even stuck to her chin hairs. The master ignored her.

狗

XIV. Backwards and with High Heels[7]

A woman decided to teach her dog to do tricks. Each day at the appointed hour she poured her energy into speaking various commands to the dog and pushing and pulling the dog into a variety of positions she wished him to take. No matter how hard she tried, the dog would not take these positions of his own accord.

One day, when she had nearly given up and thought the dog quite stupid, the dog approached her:

"Mistress," said the dog, " I thank you for all of your wonderful teaching but I am not certain if you wish me to perform these many tricks in any particular order. Please advise." With that he quickly demonstrated the entire repertoire perfectly backwards, forwards and standing on his head.

狗

XV. Non-Violence

A very strong little Spaniel dog was walking on a pleasant beach one morning. The sun was out and the sand was warm. Every smell was delicious. Suddenly, another dog, all puffed up with importance, appeared from behind a rock. It was a Beagle. He snarled at the Spaniel. "We don't allow Spaniels on this beach. Go back where you belong.." The Spaniel stood still, breathing easily, and politely allowed the beagle to finish his speech. Then he proceeded on the walk exactly as he had planned.

狗

XVI. Inner Idiot

A dog was plagued by constant interruptions in his thought by a inner idiot. The inner idiot told the dog that he was old and useless and beyond learning new tricks. One day the dog told his inner idiot "thankyou very much for your opinion," then he bit it really hard. It was the last the inner idiot was heard from.

狗

XVII. Frying Pan to Fire

A dog had been left in a car while his master went shopping. The dog was perfectly cool, though she convinced herself that the car was hot. She had water and some snacks and the window was open. The real problem was that the dog mourned the absence of her master. She managed to squeeze out the open window in order to go in search of the master. However, this particular town did not have high tolerance for dogs off leash. She was quickly apprehended and brought to the police station. No one there spoke dog. No one there understood that her motives were pure. She was a stranger in a strange land and understood her mistake but too late.

狗

XVIII. (Her) Pride Cometh Before (His) Snooze

A dog was the pride and joy of her mistress. He had been taught many tricks. He could sit, roll over, play dead, shake hands and jump through hoops. He did all the tricks quite well. One day the mistress invited her friends to her home in order to witness the dog. With great fanfare, the dog was introduced. The dog lay down and slept for two hours.

狗

XIX. No Praise No Blame[8]

A dog was always praised by his human companion. He was praised for sitting, for staying, and for coming when called. "Good boy, what a good boy," she said to him. The dog worried that this praise would feed his ego and hinder his spiritual practice. He went to his human companion. "How can I practice modesty in all things yet be the receiver of all this praise?" The companion replied, "It won't hurt you if you don't listen,."

狗

XX. Heaven and Hell[9]

A large, strong dog approached his master one day. "Master," he said, "I want to know is it true as some humans say that there is a heaven and a hell?" The master began to ridicule the dog. "You call yourself a dog? What a feeble excuse for a dog you are! You are a weak and feeble being. You have no backbone. You have no stamina. You are useless." The dog became furious. He bared his teeth and lunged toward the master. "Ah," said the master, "Here opens the gates of Hell." The dog backed off and sat down again, a bit sheepishly. "Ah," said the master, "Here opens the gates of Heaven."

狗

XXI. Emptiness

There was a dog who loved to eat. Whatever else he was doing he was easily distracted by the smell of food. He was distracted by the thought of food. One day he looked at his bowl. It was empty. He was instantly enlightened.

狗

XXII. Chinese Dogs

One day an American dog was travelling in Hubei
Province. He noticed that the little Pekinese there
traveled the streets without collars or leashes and with
no clear association with any human beings. They did
not seem to ever beg or grab food from vendors on
the streets. They did not fight or bark or interfere
with one another. They seemed happy to wander
about apparently in the company of only their own
thoughts. It came to him suddenly that he had learned
to be the kind of dog he was. He returned to his
home to think about that.

狗

XXIII. Forget About It

A very nice yellow dog had been taught as a puppy to
be submissive to humans to the point that she cow-
ered and squealed, as if she had been stepped upon,
every time a person looked her in the eye. Her new
owner was much distressed by this behavior. The
dog's cry seemed to be one of pain. The owner tried
and tried to teach the dog to stand up for herself. She
praised her when she sat straight up. She praised her

when she did not squeal. But the dog still performed a kow tow of agony with regularity. One day, the dog was chasing a ball. She became so involved in the game that she forgot that she was afraid of humans. She forgot to be anxious about meeting a person's gaze. She ran and played and fetched and brought the ball back to lots of people who were in the park that day. She did not cower and squeal.

XXIV. Learning to Hunt
When it seems there is nothing to be heard, listen. When it seems there is nothing to be seen, look.

Further Reading or Viewing

Les chiens, aussi by Azouz Beggag
Un Chien Andalou (An Andalusian Dog, Luis
Bunuel/Salvador Dali 1928)
All the Dogs in My Life by Elizabeth Von Armin
Colter by Rick Bass

Endnotes

1. Robert Gardner, as noted in the text, opened many a dog's eye, with his theory of multiple intelligences.
2. Thanks to St. Ignatius of Loyola.
3. Apologies to Deepak Chopra whose books have been an influence.
4. Based on a story told by Anthony de Mello, S.J.
5. Based on a Zen Buddhist tale.
6. Based on a story told by Anthony de Mello, S.J.
7. The reference here is, of course, to Ginger Rogers.
8. Based on a story told by Anthony de Mello, S.J.
9. Based on a Zen Buddhist tale.

About the Author

Photo Credit: Kabby Mitchell

LLyn De Danaan is an anthropologist and emerita member of the faculty, The Evergreen State College. She is a former Unitarian lay chaplain. She has written professionally for more than thirty years. *Conversations with the Inner Dog*, a prequel to *Koans*, was published by Hypatia-in-the-Woods Press in 2002.. Her fiction has also appeared in *Dog Nose News* and *Vox Populi*. She is available for readings and dog related events.

Acknowledgements

Thanks to Father Anthony de Mello, Cosmo, my Springer Spaniel and muse, Gregory Bateson, innumerable self-help books (which I find amusing) and books of and about koans (which I adore). Thanks to Kabir, Kabir as translated and interpreted by Robert Bly, and Hafiz. The dog koans are as informed by Sufism as by Buddhism. For my ideas about conversion, I thank James Luther Adams. For tips on discernment, I thank the original, St. Ignatius of Loyola. Special thanks to Lao Tzu and to Craig Carlson for introducing him to me many years ago.

Sandra Worthington was a keen, helpful editor and offered many helpful suggestions. Carol McKinley read the text closely and made useful comments. Other readers offered excellent suggestions. These included Susan Christian, Elspeth Pope, and Elizabeth Diffendal. Chris Mikulasek conferred on design decisions and celebrated with me each step of the way.

Elspeth Pope, on behalf of Hypatia-in-the-Woods Press, has offered unflagging support for this and other projects. I thank her deeply.

Additional copies may be ordered by
Contacting:
Hypatia-in-the-Woods Press
160 SE Lagoon Lane
Shelton, WA 98584
Or
ldedanaan2@hotmail.com

Koans for the Inner Dog
Has been printed
By Gorham Printing of Rochester, Washington.
The book was designed by LLyn De Danaan
using Microsoft Publisher Garamond.
Text pages are printed on 60 lb. natural
Exact Opaque offset. The cover is printed on
10 point white CIS with gloss lamination.